C000227529

Last Train to Ely

Also by Edward Storey

Poetry
North Bank Night
A Man in Winter
The Dark Music
A Slant of Light

Prose
Portrait of the Fen-country
Four Seasons in Three Countries
The Solitary Landscape
Call it a Summer Country
(Summer Journeys through the Fens)
Spirit of the Fens
Fen, Fire & Flood
The Winter Fens
Fen Country Christmas

Biography
A Right to Song
(A Life of John Clare)

Autobiography
Fen Boy First

Libretti
Katharine of Aragon Cantata
(Music by Barry Ferguson)
Old Scarlett
(Music by Trevor Hold)

Edward Storey

Last Train
to Ely

Signed for Jean.
with every good wish

Edward Storey

Rockingham Press

Published in 1995
by
The Rockingham Press
11 Musley Lane,
Ware, Herts
SG12 7EN

Copyright © Edward Storey, 1995

British Library Cataloguing-in-Publication Data

A catalogue record for this book
is available from the British Library

ISBN 1 873468 29 6

Printed in Great Britain
by Bemrose Shafron (Printers) Ltd,
Chester

Printed on Recycled Paper

Eastern Arts
Board Funded

For Angela

*Nothing to my way of thinking is a better proof of
a well-ordered mind than a man's ability to stop
just where he is and pass some time in his own
company.*

SENECA

*A man's work is nothing but this slow trek to
rediscover through the detours of art those two or
three great and simple images in whose presence
his heart first opened.*

ALBERT CAMUS

Acknowledgements

Several of these poems first appeared in the following magazines and anthologies: *Acumen, Envoi, The Month, Outposts, Proof, Ripley Poetry Association, Ver Poets* and *Vision On 1992* and *1993*.

'Beginner' won first prize in the Ver poets Open Competition 1993 and 'No Distances, No Grass' won first prize in the Wells Literature Festival 1993.

'Roads' and 'Survivors' were featured in one of LWT's programmes — *Literary Islands;* 'Storm-warning', 'The Knife' and 'I Think Today of One' were originally published in a volume of autobiography *Fen Boy First* (1992). 'Roads' and 'Men in Winter' also appeared in my earlier collection *The Dark Music* (1979).

'Distances' was written for the Gerald Finzi Society in memory of Joy Finzi and was set to music by Betty Roe.

My thanks to all concerned for their help and willingness to allow these pieces their place in this collection.

Contents

IV   a precarious boundary . . .

I

a temptation of shadows . . .

No Distances, No Grass

Within our boundaries was world enough.
Earth had no frontiers we wished to cross.
The fields upheld us and each daily sun
decided always where adventure was.

We watched our fathers working on the land,
the farmers' trailers wilting under corn;
then mothers in coarse aprons and large hats
riddling potatoes near an open barn.

We saw the seasons marry and unfold
through habit, ritual, or commonsense.
There was no need to question or explain
the narrow streets or meadows' bright expanse.

But when the gates were opened and the town
let half its children out to go abroad,
we lost our freedom and the skies closed in
like walls we could not climb or then break down.

The world was suddenly too small and old,
there were no distances, no grass, no air.
The furrows, rivers, games and days of light
were in a country we had known elsewhere.

As exiles then we told ourselves that we
were driven out like tenants with bad debts,
when what we know is that we chose to go
and being wrong is what we can't accept.

The River-Maker

The dyker who with muscle and spade
cleaved a life-line in a barren land,
gave also of his manliness to make
grain grow where water had been paramount.

How blindly did he work to one man's plan
to drain the wildfowl's roosting-place?
As bones ached with the winter's cramp
could he smell the wealth that would never be his?

More often he went to his bed with eyes
clouded by ooze from a dying fen,
no coins clutched in arthritic hands,
no lark-song lifting his head to the sun.

Grown old with delving, wracked with damp,
he'd barely strength to leave his seed
in the unwilling womb, and when he did
his child cried with the fears of darkness in its head.

But he, and a thousand of his kind,
were the beginnings and makers of this earth
which fed men's children for three hundred years
putting this note of praising in my breath.

Before these fields are drowned by iron and brick,
or farms become a new world's wilderness,
let these words ring in furrows for a man
who first made rivers glisten with December stars.

Beginner

Sometimes I think I hear the thud of your spade
striking into the mud with the slow beat
of a dying heart — a death-bell's measured stroke
tolling under a dark sky for the end of an old earth.

Each mile of dyke is a grave for that dour breed
who inhabited England — dwellers of the true Fens
where men and reed-bed, eel and bittern,
were holy relics in a land no man had conquered.

I also hear the gutteral accent of your voice
as you curse the day you were brought to work
in this kingdom of ague and mist, where men
tore out your eyes or broke your back for another's sake.

The laments you gathered from the hills, the songs
learnt from the seas, still weigh on your tongue.
I feel the longing for what you will never regain,
the sad blood mourning for a stolen house.

But all histories pass and the seed of your seed
flourished under the uninhibited skies
of a country fashioned by man's sweat —
water to water, ash to ash, flower and root.

Yet night and the silence can never forget
the resentment you felt in your labourer's chains,
or the peculiar weave of eccentric fate
that made a virtue of your unwritten elegies.

I, who am last of the first of that ken,
sing now for the sake of the land you won —
rivers out of the flood, gold from the earth,
and of days unfettered by a master's wrath.

Stiltmen

Darkness before darkness.
How on such a day could they find light
or stir from the grey ashes of their fires
a bright song? Light has no greater power
to isolate than this grim mist
which is not earth or water but a grip
holding each hour in its fist.

When they sought comfort from old hearths
they walked on stilts into what was
and is unknown for most of us. They stalked
through fen and flood to find those cures
as secret as the grave. More
than in birth or death there is a force
which beckons and a curse that lures.

Darkness beyond darkness
still clogs up the mind like mud on wheels
which, turning, only grind a deeper rut
into the soil that should first heal
and then bear fruit. How can seeds explode
or wings find air without new light? Toil
is without a cause unless some hands applaud.

Shadows

Here where the land cranes its thick neck
to stare beyond the water-line, we walk
on stilts to give our spirits height
and stride on legs which lift our weight
above the reedy bog. You'd think
such striving for the light would spunk
our limbs to struggle for the sun
more eagerly than those whose bourn
is half-way there. Not so!
We're frightened too of what we do not know.
More effort is required to keep
our bodies raised. We need the cup
of praising if we must look
at things of which we dare not speak.

Living below the level of the sea
gives us the benefit of greater sky
in which to reach for light, but space
can terrify and in our eyes
you'll see the fear of distances.
Yes, we are afraid of boundaries.
Safer to walk this land where clouds
crouch on horizons, where clods
glisten with ancient peat soaked
by the rain. A man who's looked
upon this land knows his own mind.
If we attempt to rise above the ground
it is to see with sharper eye
the contours of the earth. Maybe
we are afraid, not of the light or sun,
but of those shadows trying to get in.

Roads

Here there is always a long way to go.
The roads do not encourage you into
deceptive corners or an enticing ridge
as they do in hill-country. On this edge
of earth's platform they beckon beyond
a few trees or farmhouse, separating a land
that sulks below sea-level. Look any way
and these roads narrow towards the sky,
towards that space where the clouds grow.
You can take these roads at their face value,
they have nothing to hide and what you cannot see
is beyond the boundary of the naked eye.

You may feel that a man's stature should be measured
by his landscape, his bones hard, his fissured
brow a replica of the rock's forehead,
the contours' rhythm caught in his stride.
Not here. A man gauges his worth against
intemperate winds, feeling his face rinsed
by the rain flung in from the sea. He works
not by stone walls but by those open dykes
where rats nest in the soft peat and eels
slip through the dark stream like a vague thought.
You can hate these roads or find, like hills,
they lift you, step by step, out of the soul's drought.

Man and Winter

For the first time this winter
the fields are salted with frost,
the black soil silent again
after the chant of the plough
and white procession of gulls.

Nearby a man blows into his hands
renewing a habit that will last a season.
It is not prayer that comforts
the cold ache of his flesh but breath
warmed with his own fire.

The distance is brought nearer by mist
which seldom deserts this land
during days that hardly get started.
You need to be different to work these fields.
It's almost a calling.

Men meet times like this with blood
that has tested the worst of each year.
They too are salt, earning more
than their keep and the sun's bonus,
paying more than a rent to be part of the earth.

Landscape of Wounds

If earth's furrows were flesh
these fields would be wet
with the fresh blood of wounds
cleaved by the plough, their clods
sticky and warm as limbs
throbbing with pain undressed
on some battleground. But
here where the soil is raw
and open to the winds
we do not need to carve
such images to shock the eye.
Earth has its own agony.

Today I watched two men
working their scythes
along the narrow dyke, each blade
clean as a scalpel, each stroke
keen as a surgeon's knife.
In cutting down the reeds
they let in light. Black
water suddenly was white,
not only with the sun
but with that ancient life
which pulses in the vein
even when limbs grow stiff
and death waits in the bone.

Acceptance

I watched them ploughing the frost in
to leaven the land, bright knuckles
of steel kneading the black soil —
a continuance of those tasks which
broke earth's crust and still
demand all that a man's worth.

I thought I had come to see
this transformation of the year as
dandruff on the tired shoulders
of summer. Yet today the fields
are laid-out, groomed and brushed
not for a funeral but for a birth.

Grey beards of reed twitch in the sun
with the unshaken faith of Simeon.
For them, no more than sleep separates
winter from spring. But what will
rise out of the dark, or burst
from this buried frost then?

Such questions they need never ask.
They plough on while the light lasts,
leaving philosophy to those
who cannot accept that some seeds
die, some germinate; that what survives
is all that next year grows.

Winter is Only

There was once a reason
for returning to these fields.
Even in winter their soil gave hints
of something called Spring.
Now they are laid out
like the corpse of an old man,
his nostrils stuffed with snow,
his veins stiff with ice.
Why does he not stir
when I kick him on the shin,
or twitch when I stick
my pen into his arm?

But which is dead — the vision
or the limb? The heart or head?
Why do these fields of snow
no longer show the promises
which once they had? I stare
across the furrows and recall
all that was prophecied,
all that has come to be.
Now I need more than sun
or the quick and physical
experience of love.
Winter is only of the young.

Once

    Beneath the soil,
skin-deep for this day's measurement,
remains the memory of a sea
long before boundaries or shores
decided who should plunder or betray.

    Beneath that sea
from which our world was built
there was the ice that separated
land from land and bred a chasm in the bed
of more than rock or tribe.

    Beneath the ice
there was a fire which raged all winter
in the bone. Given its chance
it leapt about and proved
beneath the calm exterior of man

    there roamed a beast
which, born beneath the boggy waste
before the sun had cracked its seed,
gave birth to violence in the blood
before the heart had time to ache.

    Before the fire
there was the void in which all stillness
had its rest. Where then the voice
that woke the seed and stirred
all history into lust? Somewhere
between the word and deed, design was lost.

Survivor

Black on black
the colour deepens beyond the day
to show another world held back
upon the furrowed page when earth
was wrinkled more by water than the plough,
where men expressed themselves in breath
heaved into air by limbs that knew
no other comfort that the sleep
which entered into them with night.

Today one man survives to show
how time has passed him by,
almost forgotten him within the light
that filters from a sky grown old
with watching. So burdened now with pain
he does not raise an eye
or lift his head from toil
to see what caused the shadow
darkening the soil.

Below the level of the dyke,
where water glistens closer to the sun
than his moist eye can reach,
he bends over the spade's clogged hilt,
his braces strained across his back
with all the tautness of a catapult.
But he's too solid and root-fixed
to know the joy of stone
shot briefly out of sight.

He is both past and present,
birth and death, the blood and spittle
of ten thousand years that raised
his place in history from beast —

to what? Should we regret
his breath has done no more
than leave an image on our winter sky
of what is certain for us all —
the shadow of a horseman passing by?

Beyond the Memory

What hibernating cell of a thousand years
suddenly woke to the sound of your voice?

It was only a brief utterance in the air,
older than the spade's thrust or the last oar

dipping into the sea. But there was a lilt
in the cadence of your song and I felt

the seed jump in my blood, your foreign tongue
made as familiar as the words I daily sang.

And so I understood why others with that gift
attracted praise, became part of the true weft,

for they had tasted the same salt-spray on the mouth,
honing their diction on the winds of the north.

I knew then that we encompass within ourselves
all that ever was and cannot change. We evolve

from something beyond the memory, carrying the past
with us. It is only the recognition that is lost,

the ability to listen in the dark to that long night
when, in another land, two lovers met

bestowing credence on a temperament and name
which have but this one needle-point to bless, or blame.

23

Last Train to Ely

Some countries can look back
and remember when they were beautiful,
their ruins reminders of days
when palaces stood on the hills
and halls gave room to the harpist.

Not here. Our wilderness recalls
a time of swamp, when men
shared winter with their animals
and dampness put a burden in the bone;
cold poverty still in their fires.

Few would have danced then
or played more than a primitive tune.
It would be truer to say that we
are the ones who have come closest
to banquet halls and the pleasures of song.

Our ruins lie beneath the soil,
stripped bare of gods or myths — black
bog-oaks and bronze-age pots
distinguished more by mud
than golden masks and hieroglyphs.

I was reminded of this today
on the last train to Ely, facing the way
I had already been, the fields
receding as the rails became
a fast re-winding of what had gone.

A stranger opposite looked out and said
'God, what a dreadful land, all muck and flood.
How anyone could live out there beats me.'
I think I understood. What could he see
not knowing what was hidden from the eye?

But if he'd looked at where the plough
had turned the furrows round for spring
he would have noticed tracks of lighter shade
where rivers once obeyed a natural flow
before that land was drained.

Those veins of ancient silt
speak of a time when fens were wild
with boar and bittern, wolves and geese.
Beneath their map exists another world
as old as that we seek to find in Greece.

And someone once, I thought,
first led that tribe in song
however hoarse the wind. So I have come
on this last run from places never sought,
to find my travelling out is always going home.

Afterwards

It is finished. The year's labours
have been folded away like linen
into the drawers of winter —
a starched table-cloth of field
all that remains now the feast is over.

Crumbs of snow litter the grass
by dykeside and river; water and sky
ironed into each other's shadow.
Frost tightens its knot on flesh
and furrow. Here death has no cover.

Hands which delved into the land
for profit or sorrow must warm
themselves by a short day's fire.
Sleep is only a limited season;
this famine will not last forever.

II

the first shudder of the turning tide . . .

I Think Today of One

I think today of one who
even before her childhood was quite done
worked in the fields in frost and sun
from day's first light until the moon
sent labourers home, the girls
to mend torn garments in a lamp-lit room
made private by the pulling down of blinds.

Then, when the cockerels called
or neighbours knocked upon her window-pane,
she went with others just as young
back to the farm, her slender form
ill-matched for such long toil,
having no time to watch the tall
slow cumulus or hear the skylark's dirl.

And yet through her I love this land
where less appeals to unperceiving eyes
than what I find. I know I take
the aches and elements at second-hand
and should regret that she
was forced by circumstance to break
her spirit where I forge my song. But who

will understand the meaning of
my labours now unless they honour hers?
She would be quick to contradict
my pity and explain in simple terms
that others had fared worse.
She kept her thoughts like secrets in a house
where sorrows should be patched behind closed doors.

Snap-shot

Was she that young, once? If only
I could breathe on the photograph
and bring her back to life, make water move
and ripple round her feet, she might
step out to prove she was a girl who
liked to laugh and run along the beach,
slender as grass and gossamer-light;
each day a gift — wife, mother, daughter, son
caught by the camera many tides ago
when holidays were brief and summers won
out of long months of servitude.

Why is it when we see ourselves
as children, our parents look no younger
than today? as if we are the only ones
who grow, while they stay ageless, until
a certain moment shatters that calm pose
and suddenly the sea, smiles, years,
dry-up into these wrinkles of tired skin
that now hangs loosely on the bone
and can so easily be bruised
when memory no longer drugs with lies
and pictures hurt as only home-truths can.

Smoke Signals

My father, who'd not smoked for forty years,
    sat on his death-bed puffing mock cigars
and blowing smoke-rings down the midnight ward
    like tiny haloes flying without wings.

He did not speak but smiled and gently waved
    at someone opposite who was not there.
The pain had left him as his mind returned
    to days when he was young, with strength to spare.

Within his tight-skinned skull already cold
    he felt the sun and heard the laughing sea
where he'd gone paddling on his one week off,
    his work-day trousers rolled up to the knee.

I tried to talk but something in my throat
    choked back the words for I was now a child
clutching his hand as I did then, afraid
    of what might happen should I lose my hold.

I watched his fingers stiffen round my own,
    his staring eyes withdraw, the smoke-rings fade.
And, in the low-lit ward beyond his death,
    felt the first shudder of the turning tide.

The Knife

'How sharp is it now?' I asked
when you had honed your knife-blade
on a pumice-stone kept for that
purpose in the kitchen drawer.

Stretching your forearm out, you cut
a swath clean through the growth of hair,
like someone cutting corn, then said
'It's sharp enough, I think. You try.'

I lightly drew the knife along your arm
afraid that I might cut too deep and hurt.
But it was not your flesh that bled,
and only now I feel the wound.

Deceptions

What brought the smell of boarding-houses back
I cannot say. The air was hot and lathery as soap,
    when suddenly the room felt full of presences
      and there we stood, as shadowy as smoke.

And half the day was changed because one sense
picked up the odour of a place where holidays were spent
    when I was six. There, on a sultry afternoon,
      I saw myself a child again, transfixed.

I watched my father first unpack each case,
then mother test the wash-jug on its stand. I did not know
    one week could last so long, or fifty years be lost
      as summers are in mislaid photographs.

Somewhere the sea was waiting, while the house
(with musty walls and many-patterned stains) reminded us
    its rooms were built for strangers who would not
      be staying longer than a week, though smell remains.

I climbed on to a chair to see how near
we were to beaches, waves and rocks. Too far I fear to get
    full benefit from days I'd lived for all the year;
      I knew at six how disappointments hurt.

I closed my door, knowing how easily
we let such distances outstrip a need to be elsewhere,
    for when I smelt again that sea-world weight of salt,
      I was the only one left standing there.

The Same Man

So, to you, the last seed-planter
to receive from a tired lip
this late moment of praise,
know that the player has found
a tune that would bring you home
to a familiar sound in a cramped room.

Days use us as the wind and rain
choose to undo all that we plan,
and I have waited too long to explain
why the song you brought to birth
blew itself out before the music began.
Each promise is a fragile, tenuous thing.

How could I value your gift then
when I knew nothing of love's worth?
A father tries too hard to make his son
into the man he would have been
but fails because the child is older than
one generation's breath or parent's wrath.

Today I saw your last-born standing where
you'd also stood — marriage and death
uniting us in blood's allegiances.
You were both young and old, seen and unseen,
a memory caught like some forgotten air
played on a cornet in the afternoon.

And I was the outsider who
could not hide the tears which grieve
for eyes that wept three hundred years ago.
You were the man whose shadow barred the path
between what was and is, and by
love's shackles, would not let me leave.

In Going Back to What's No Longer There

Whether it would ever be the same for me
    I cannot say. I try to imagine
existing in another country but know,
    for whatever reason, the heart would stay
fixed in that land where more than memory
    claws at my brain. Again and again
I am hauled back to a familiar stream,
    to fields, voices, streets and rooms
where a child lived, not so much for himself
    as for others, like a tree's new leaf.
There dream was fact and elsewhere lacked reality.

But you have known the tearing up of roots,
    with windows broken and the doors condemned.
How, then, can you return without each wound
    re-opening itself, each distant sound
re-echoing in your head — the talk, cries,
    shouts and jack-boots in the night
loud in your ears? Ghosts mock the years
    that separate and claim allegiance
exile asked as rent. So love is always torn
    when two demand of one all that is spent.
Hearts cannot choose what colder choice denies.

In going back to what's no longer there
    we must return to being what we are
and find in darkness each lost room of light
    where days had other joys than those events
scorched on earth's calendar. All that we learn
    in seeking what is past is that our birth
is closer to a death. When that is reached
    we cannot change the legacy or fate
stamped on our flesh. Our paths are set.
    The roots remain unsevered and the stream
in which we swam no one can now pollute.

'The Meeting House'

There they go, in ones and twos
through the unmelting snow of a Victorian England,
their dark meeting-place wedged like a glacier
between tall brooding houses. Who lies
unrisen in the burial-ground no one can say;
headstones make boundaries which separate
the living from the dead, and those unseen
are permanent guests of winter.

The living move in silence towards a door
through which a weak light shines.
That light divides the watching from the watched,
guarding old secrets from the frozen earth.
Like question-marks, two people passing by
stare at the few who struggle after truth;
a woman and her dog pause near a tree
and from a half-closed curtain, eyes accuse.

Nearby are iron-railings and a gate,
a northern wall of stone still capped with snow;
but something else puts barriers between
the ones who trust and those who walk away.
This painting in its silence says it all,
there are no answers to the questions asked.
No matter how much cold consumes our day
a deeper frost destroys their ritual now.

After the Funeral

Perhaps only the dead hear
    though many listen.
Words fail again to fill
    the spaces between stones.
They or the speaker were
    the wrong ones chosen
        for this death's undertones.

We never know until
    each cold dejection
how empty is a day
    so full of grief. Eyes weep
as some eyes always will
    for each occasion.
        (Unwept eyes seldom sleep).

Some words are only meant
    for those beyond earth's ways —
a voice sent into silence
    for which there are no walls.
The public tribute spent
    in vain, why seek for praise
        if flattery appals?

We honour best the dead
    with quieter elegies
that have no echoes in
    a vaulted roof. There is
a language left unsaid
    for those who mourn true loss.
        Such grief needs no excuse.

Leaves

And bugles answered, sorrowful to hear.
                    WILFRED OWEN

You could call it peace — the yellow leaves
of lime trees shedding a November day.
It's a cold stillness but not without power
to move more than a season. Light weaves
a silent elegy through branches which give way
to the black seal of winter. Within an hour
the dying foliage will shield more earth than sky
and other fallings now disturb the memory.

It was a day like this when we first stood
on fields where half a generation fell
less slowly than the leaves, less willingly
than shadows. Each year we count its blood
in petals and make the tolling of a bell
postpone the darker threat that chillingly
stares back at us from unbuilt cenotaphs.
No stone is large enough to bear those griefs.

And there are others too who contradict
all thoughts of beauty. Autumn is full
of unkind images. How can the days forget
when bullet, bomb and fire conspire to evict
the innocent from what for them was beautiful?
The stillness grows more tense. There is regret
even in peace that makes the leaves express
not only joy but each heart's emptiness.

Then let the season change, let winter come
and bury under snow all mockeries
that offend, all promises unmade.
The trees are bare, the fallen leaves are dumb,
and there's an end to each year's prophecies
as one by one intentions are betrayed.
Street-lamps shed pools of light on paths made sad
with evening, and those most living are the dead.

Dusk

There is this hour of the forgotten stones
when shadows come as much from underground
as from the sun. But it's too late to count
the names once sacred there. The bones are now
dry relics stripped of love. They wait
not for a resurrection but the sound
of concrete changing ownership with grass.
  This is the hour of all the grief there was.

There is a place where at this common time
light fades from narrow windows in a church
where coloured glass still serves to mark a sill
like pages in a book no longer read —
a thread of silence laid across the dust,
the musty smell of liturgies now dead.
They built these stones to reach beyond the grave.
  This is the place where only shadows move.

There is a land where from both bomb and shell
a darkness falls before the daylight ends.
Old women die and children lose their legs
watched by the world through t.v's hungry lens.
And others live their hell where fatter flies
crawl in and out of mouths that are not fed;
their eyes grown big from what they've never known.
  This is a land where love is seldom seen.

There is a time when nothing more will hold,
when shadows fill the streets and secret lanes,
where innocence is blown to smithereens
because some cheaper god is on its throne.
We walk at dusk through what remains of earth,
through scenes where wisdom is already spent.
The prophecies we mocked are now fulfilled.
  This is the time we feared, the child we killed.

A Preparation

Where will the freed bird settle, what search for,
when the ribbed bars of its cage bend or buckle
     in the heat of the estranging sun?

There is a lifetime's choice of many rooms
waiting under the ashes of stars. Break all
     the ruined windows or locked-doors down

it will rebuild each house, each crumbled wall
to find its perch, the spoon-latch of a place where
     wings broke from their shell and old men toiled.

First it will seek the parched hand of a woman
still chair-bound by an empty grate, her face
     disturbed from sleep by the singer's flight,

then turn, as other have before, to find no more
than summer's boarding-house, knowing it owns
     an everlasting season in its throat.

There are alternatives. A house by the sea's edge
where waves once watched a blind boy drown,
     or rooms where silence was enshrined

in a polished table with its vase of flowers.
Or it could be a hill where strangers tried
     to raise a rough child on wild nectarines,

or in that country where forbidden eyes
disguised their secrets and betrayed the vows
     all lovers make by candle-flame.

But none will ever equal those great skies
where light is permanent and wings have grace
     to rise like larks above the commonplace.

III

some other distances . . .

Loss

The queen's room has been stripped bare,
its walls no more than an empty tomb
where all that was part of her reign
has gone to pay the ferryman's fare.

Nothing remains but her presence here
in the shadows cast by a weeping sun.
Fruit lies bruised in September grass,
death echoes again each mortal fear.

Through her long widowhood she strove
to keep her young king's name alive —
and what the world remembers now
is immortality born of love,

not just for a man and the songs he made
but for all the beauty that he praised.
So fine a hand, so true an eye
never before had flesh displayed.

Such grief was not a common pain
worn on the sleeve of a courtly dress.
It was the celebration of a gift
flowering after the winter's rain.

And who can share her loneliness
without that darkest kiss? Love knows
no greater agony than loss,
sorrow no deeper wound than this.

Distances

For J.F.

It is not death that separates but love;
a house has emptiness grief cannot fill —
some hearts have distances no eyes can prove.

I knew a boy who walked towards his trove
where moonlight hid the crazy waves that kill;
it is not death that separates but love.

Once there was music that could always move
despair from night; it cannot do so still —
some hearts have distances no eyes can prove.

And there were gardens with an apple grove
where younger laughter lit each summer hill;
it is not death that separates but love.

I knew a man who innocently strove
towards a dream he thought fate would fulfil —
some hearts have distances no eyes can prove.

Days, like old rooms, have shadows where we hove
clutching a hand late winters cannot chill.
It is not death that separates but love —
some hearts have distances no eyes can prove.

Lost Days

It is the distance that brings you close,
    as though a river over-flowed
and lapped its water at this house
which several counties separate
    from the familiar boundaries.

Here there are no horizons. The sky's
    no more than a frieze for roofs
that block out light. Walls tremble
at the wind's cry, squinting an eye
    at the wild swans' incredible flight.

I can feel tonight your cold hands
    touching again that nerve
caught in the rib's claw and know
I should have stayed where there's no need
    to ask who is the betrayer, the betrayed?

There is some balm in the recurring thought
    that you will never let me down,
never fail to forgive the old flaw
in the soul's structure, or turn away
    from a man begging in unfamiliar streets.

Message

But who will know?
Words are spent on the wind,
torn, frayed like sheep's wool
on the bare thorns of a hedge;
lodge in the branches of a tree.

I walk over the land
in a direction of my own choosing.
Eyes look at clouds, ears
listen to larks; but the tears
were not chosen, nor the stone in the heart.

What I say to the sky
or shout into air, is lost —
like the cock's crow mocking
a man's lie. Why must truth
be hollered in vain from the day's throat?

It is enough that you
will find this note left on the shelf
of a year where too many seasons
were crammed into spring. Read it
and hear what only can be said in silences.

Scenes from Edward Hopper

They are all asking the same questions — the girl
sitting alone at night at a restaurant table,
her hat shading her eyes in artificial light,
her hands unable to lift the cup beyond
her emptiness. And there's a man who sits alone
each Sunday morning outside a vacant shop,
a brooding shadow on the side-walk's step,
like someone heard half-talking in his sleep.

And here an usherette is waiting by the stairs
for strangers to arrive and claim the dreams
for which the cinema was built. It's all the same.
The rows are full of ghosts, her torch unlit.
And others share a room but are made separate
by distances — she at a piano, fingering one note,
he with his paper, but both divided by a door
that has no means by which to open it.

Elsewhere, an ageing couple in a quaint hotel
wait for attention. No one hears the bell.
From their appearance one might well assume
arrival — or departure? Who can tell?
For them it is the moment in between. Each
with the other, both sadly on their own
preparing for a time when only one will be
standing alone, a coat held on the arm.

Rooms look anonymous, like something lent.
Light makes each shadow stark, as if it meant
to isolate the needs of those seeking escape.
Apartment blocks have squares from which eyes stare,
not wanting to look out but rather to look in.
And still the faces ask 'What is it for? Where
did it all go wrong? How long can this night last?'
There's nowhere else to go when answers never come.

Four Poems on Edward Hopper Paintings

1. A Middle-aged Couple

Her dreams are now in a book,
his on the empty railway track
outside their room. Once
they were shared and ran towards
a common meeting-place long since
un-met — their travelling marred
by incidents unplanned, each
settling for a station they could reach.

She sits, half-dressed. He stands
close to the window for his cigarette.
There is no hurry for the middle-aged.
They wait and think about what was
or is — a something in between
that both unites and separates.
There's always time to dress, undress,
accept, reject, adjust to loneliness.

She turns the pages slowly. He
glances at the ash held in his hand.
Another night, day, journey done,
another hotel room, the jug
of water stale now on its stand.
No need for explanations.
Once more on walls the shadows prove
the sun remains outside, like love.

2. *Office Clerk*

A man sits at his empty desk
staring out at the day's light.
It's not the future that he sees
but rather the past — all that might
have been if only the first risk
had been taken. There are no trees
on the skyline, only the flat
rooftops in a shaded street —
and all those questions windows make us ask.

The walls are bare. Even the sun
succeeds only in leaving a square
of blankness where no shadows fall.
There is no other being there,
no laughter heard, no movement seen,
only the silence of a tall
building when everyone has gone.
Yet he remains, brooding alone,
knowing the key of darkness will turn soon.

3. The Chair

If this chair were suddenly vacant
everything would still be there
except the girl sitting by the window —
the table with its vase of flowers
nearest the light; the velvet cloth
neatly arranged by hand; the blinds
partly pulled down to shade the sun.

Across the street the houses would sleep on
throughout the drowsy afternoon,
each secret life hidden in shadow.
Even the chair would still exist,
a piece of furniture within a room
full of its former presences, as if
it waited for the girl's return.

Perhaps there's no such thing as emptiness
but varying degrees of light and shade
that hide, reveal, like curtains drawn
to separate us from the world outside.
In every stillness there must be
something we cannot touch but only feel,
for when we look again the chair is occupied.

4. Morning

She, too, sits there
trying to make sense
of an empty room.

The walls are bare,
the bed on which she slept
stripped of its sheets.

An open window
lets in morning light.
She feels its warmth.

But what of night?
Was she alone? Her eyes
stare out of dreams

with such regret,
such distance in the head,
we must assume

the only shadow
which she could have shared
is now invisible.

Pietà

(From a bronze by Käthe Kollwitz)

The man returns as a child
to rest within the thighs from which he came;
his legs bent double, his head thrown back,
as helpless as a creature newly born.

The mother's pain is greater at his death
than anything she felt at birth.
Then the fulfilment eased her suffering
and no one saw the star shaped as a cross.

Today her grief is burdened
with the apparent failure of a dream,
sobs heaving with the sorrow of a heart
asking repeatedly 'What have they done?'

She aches to take him back
into herself, the first fruit of her womb
lying so bruised and lifeless in her lap,
till loneliness itself becomes a wound.

All she can be is the warm cradle
in which his body sleeps — a woman
rocking her baby through the night;
her tears falling as balm upon his brow.

Her Eyes Remain Cold Sorrows

(From a sketch by Käthe Kollwitz)

More shadows than light
because some greys are always permanent.

Corners fill out the room,
the day is still a paler shade of night.

A woman sits the other side of hope
staring into the ashes of a dream.

Upon the table is a knife,
and on the chair-back hangs a waiting rope.

What burden could be worse
than being a poor woman, mother, wife?

Her flesh is bloodless,
each dry breast folded like an empty purse.

But somewhere in the dark
a child sleeps on. A husband prays for work.

'While there is life ...' How trite!
Her eyes remain cold sorrows. Memories mock.

Where is the wine of love,
the promised comfort of the broken bread?

She cups her hands to grieve,
to drown the cries of hunger in her head.

All the Colours of Grey

(From the drawings of Käthe Kollwitz)

i

I did not see it then and, only now
    through other eyes older than mine,
        begin to recognise those poverties.

The room is dark. The fire in the grate
    almost burnt out. Feelings are stretched
        not out of hate but from love's ironies.

There is a bed, a chair, a candle flame.
    And in the streets a wasting child
        with nothing but a name, testing death's boundaries.

Your hollow eyes are drained of tears
    for you have wept from hunger and from grief
        beyond all fears and failing promises.

There is no bread; no milk left in your breast.
    Night still persists. Silence, like waiting,
        is a wound at best, mocking all tenderness.

ii

Silence, like waiting, is a wound
    and, without hope, an emptiness
        that crouches in the shadows of a house.

And you are there — wife, mother, girl,
    bewildered by the burden of it all.
        If this is life, you ask, what use of toil?

A man comes home — lover, husband, tool
   of the better off; dispensable,
      his pockets empty. How can he console?

Your child then trespasses too close to death
   and you are left with nothing but your grief.
      There are no words to shape his epitaph.

The room is colder now. The light,
   like prying eyes from curtains, is withdrawn.
      You feel the air grow heavier than stone.

iii

The light, like prying eyes, now knows
   enough. The lids are closed. Your hands
      wring out the darkness like a cloth.

Two share one helplessness — a loss
   with nothing said and only love's brief touch
      that brings poor comfort to you both.

All language is "too narrow and too weak
   to ease us now; great sorrows cannot speak."
      Hope was made bankrupt by a child's last breath.

Then what will be beyond despair? For death
   only begins what is no longer there.
      There is no room for pity, only wrath.

Earth writes its own obituary. You saw,
   before my eyes were opened, what would be.
      Then let us weep in silence, angrily.

A Postscript to Shostakovitch's Reply

I hear the music of the dead from a great distance,
not the voices of the known but of the unknown
who died under snow, or of an infamous hunger.

Speechless, they speak now in your music —
cries torn on the wind, tears blown into splinters.
Out of the grey sky I see their arms, thin as rain.

Such music comes from a long suffering
and how can we know pain who have not felt
the torturer's iron, or weep if we've not seen
the bones of children swept into the street?

Then let it rain all winter on this land
for nothing now can drown the voices of the dead
who cry within the comfort of my room
or in shocked eyes defy the hollowness of stars.

IV

a precarious boundary . . .

On Looking at Your Painting
of Ely Cathedral

(For Tony Porter)

You have lifted the stones towards the sun
and filled the lantern with new light,
your tower as luminous as the leaves
thrown out of focus on each branch.
I let my eyes rise with the mist that gives
an opaque look to solid things
and lures me into thinking, inch by inch,
this church has no foundation, only wings.

There is a quality of fine stained-glass
through which the mind explores beyond
the darkened window and the tree, to find
a greater light behind the stone.
Because your vision is their root
leaf, branch and tower all illuminate.

Ash Wednesday

This day, more than was known
by those whose gifts were greater than
my years demand, is still my own;
earth-life more priceless than the works of man.

Snow threatens, my words have gone blind.
Ambition almost ceases to exist.
There is a different hunger in the mind.
I am, so far, the one death missed.

Pierce then the hide of sky
and let this ageing skin express
what is, turning a brighter eye
on what was once earth's emptiness.

Beyond this sack-cloth day
is yet more breath, love, hope — yes, joy!

Gifts

Why, being bountiful, benevolent
as the giver of all you ask,
then take away the sweetness of each gift
and let love sour, expose to risk
the frailty of innocence? Must we,
the beneficiaries of love,
suffer because of being what you made
and, like first-fathers, live to grieve?

But then I heard your advocate explain
true gifts betoken trust and come
with no intent to punish or malign.
Self-greed abuses and bears shame.
Be satisfied that what you have received
will last, bless, multiply, ungrieved.

The Source

How ever briefly
it is the energy
within the moment of silence
that makes the flame
burn most fiercely.
It is the mind's power
that transforms darkness
into light, swifter
than the touched switch,
briefer than a struck match.
It is the split second
when God's hand
rests on the seed of death .
and, from its fire,
forges a new birth.
Within a skull is the one
temple that can house
each miracle. We fall
only as stars fall to prove
the frailty of stone.

What Then?

You will find out, said God.
So use this day to unwrap
my gift from the shroud
of your own making. Keep
faith with all you were taught.
What will be, when your body
shadows the hill, should not
make you less greedy
for breath bought by my blood.
Guilt fathers fear more than
a diagnosis of what is bad.
Remember, I too was a man.
If you are to forgive those
who will pay for your pardon,
forgive yourself this
old, unnecessary question.
I gave you life. Then
shed your thoughts of death
and from my cup of wine
subdue all wrath.

Some Call it Peace

It is always there,
the old hunger for what cannot be found
in the false light of a rented room
or under the brash sun of a deconsecrated sky.

Beneath the clamour of bells
a voice speaks, quietly as an eye
raised in the direction of someone admired
and we recognise it for its own true note.

Some call it peace.
For some it is the brief awakening of self
buried for years under the weight
of wrong decisions and unfortunate mistakes;

an old longing for what was
before we took to wearing masks
and listening to the trinkets' vulgar chimes.
But, what is always there, cannot be lost.

There are those days when light
breaks through the skin and we regain
a moment of that time which Adam knew
before his eyes were opened — and he was blind.

Faith

Even at this lateness,
when eyes become weary
of searching for answers,
it is still hard to believe
our strength comes in the waiting,
that the only song worth breathing on
is the one sleeping in stone,
stretching its limbs slowly
like a child aware of the womb's weakness
to keep it forever from uncertain light.

Until Stone Becomes Water

There is still a cave in the garden
where the immediate wounds are healed
by the ointment of love; the inevitable
waiting between dying and dying.
The mob has gone back to its trading
in wares that destroy the spirit.
Only the faithful remain, gathering herbs
to soothe more than a week's sorrow,
knowing that love did not deserve
the gash in its side, or a barbed wreath.

But who has the muscle to move that weight
which prevents the sun rising? Limbs
will not dance nor eyes fill with light
until stone becomes water, and tears bear fruit.

The Tree

Let it be so.   If
out of the unassuaged hunger
some other bread is given
to satisfy the heart's need,
why turn away with hands
empty, the face sullen
as a spoilt child denied
the fruits of its greed.

There are some meats
that fill for an hour,
leaving the guts blown
and the aftertaste sour.
It is wiser to live
off the one tree that knows
no seasons, or beckons not
with blossom that is false.

Expiation

Yes, if the light holds,
we shall ride into our own
Jerusalem, not to the crowds'
waving but on roads
silenced by the palms of forgiveness.

There will be rejoicing
but not out of triumph.
Our alleluias will rise
from hearts quietly grateful
that our deaths have been died for us.

We shall respect the stones
at our feet, acknowledge the jury;
but our eyes will be fixed
on that hill to which
we need not go now the cross is empty.

Light

It must give you cause to think, God,
when your gifts are traded in the back streets
of a town, when what should have been good
is besmirched by the tawdry delights
of a night that knows nothing but sin.

I think we would all understand
if your patience ran out, if despair
made you alter your plans and pretend
that we'd already gone. But may your desire
to father us all outlast even the sun.

Only in knowing that can our morning begin.

Master

Have you forgotten the flowers
and music as your spare words
spill their invisible tears
on a bare altar, or those
moments of sunlight
when a window becomes
more that a work of art
or the keyhole of thunder?
Have you forgotten the faiths
of those who came, like you,
out of the heart's need
and found in the stillness
miracles?

        You were right
to show us the scars of our sins
and smug hypocrisies, but
leave us more than your dust
and the soul's disenchantment.
Turn now from your elegies
and print on our sky
a song of triumph that will last
beyond all stone.

The Price

For the sake of a curse a crow was killed,
his dressed-in-mourning wings stretched out
like some black Christ upon a cross
but with no merit in its sacrifice.

I saw today its shining beauty spilled
from one low bough when autumn was about
and knew its death was simply to expose
the weakness of a rich man's avarice.

For the sake of that crow a tree was felled
to pay for the gunman's rifle-shot.
Crow, Christ and symbol all must lose
when thieves ride in and dying men accuse.

Dead Song

For one who under the shadow of error
wishes to sing, the notes sound false.
Words ring with the weight of a cracked bell
that has hung in the tower of a sad house
too many years without trying its tongue.
It would be easier to adjust the image
in a broken mirror than re-tune the song
of one who knows what should not have been done.

But who has not, at some time in a casual way,
stepped into a ray of unexpected light
and known the promise of a season's fruit?
Night after night there flickers on the wall
a hint of what still aches within the bone,
giving each air a sadder, wiser tone.

The Other Way

I can accept now
it is beyond the ritual of the rung bell
or candle-flames carried by neophytes
    through a choir-stall.

It is beyond too
the ceremony of sharing the bread and wine
of one often absent from his own meal
    and dining alone.

But it is so.
How can we greet the host of a house
if we shut him out from his own door
    with our raw noise?

How can we find peace
in the vulgar language of prayer, or kneel
at a crumbling rail, when what we require
    is a silence to heal?

I will take his way,
walking from stones down a holier aisle
where sky offers its own bread, where
    earth's cup is all.

Poet

In the end
    it is only the one word
        that matters. We give names
like art, gift, love
    but it is more
        than can be expressed
in syllables.

We're like the child
    whose only adjective
        for the sea was 'big'.
We have no language
    to explain the stark
        simplicity of truth
even when understood.

There was a man
    who all his life, strove
        to achieve some fame
through probing scenes of drama,
    fire and lust, when
        what he should have done
was stay at home

waiting for news.
    There is no choice if we
        would be the giver and the gift.
All else must be surrendered
    to accept the name
        we would prefer in life
as well as on our epitaphs.

Odds-on

Which of the two
will first see the light of day
        I cannot say.

Words out of air
settle like moths on the page
        from another age.

No one will say
'they're just what I'm looking for.
        Do you have more?'

I'll bury them
now in the grave of my desk
        until others ask.

Perhaps when I'm dust
they'll emerge from their chrysalis
        to prove just this —

Light and the dark
are the same, an odds-on chance
        luck might enhance.

Today they may die;
tomorrow honour my death
        with a delayed breath.

Or we may both
stay locked in a drawer, unknown,
        wingless and bone.

On the Way to a Committee-meeting of the John Clare Society

I saw an old man sitting on a stone
beside a five-barred gate, his wild eyes
staring through me as I passed, as if
I had no right to cross a world
he'd fenced with private boundaries.

His gaze had hints of madness like a fire
raked by the wind. His bulbous head
(too big for what was left of him)
crimson with threats of anger or
some vision that was burning deep inside.

The first impression was of some daft clown
turned out of house to spend the afternoon
on country roads, out of harm's way. But then
I thought he might have chosen to be there
rather than waste his presence on the sane.

Wild flowers were his company, the fields
his joy. And, for a moment, I believed
I'd seen a poet sitting by that gate.
I would have stopped the car, gone back to look ...
But in my heart I knew it was too late.

Ballad of the Railway-station Waiting-room

(For Trevor Hold)

We met, as strangers often do, and talked as friends.
He, hoping to make some kind of journey back;
I, having to travel forward, yet both
the reluctant passengers of fate.

It's dark in here, he said, *and cold. What time's
your train?* I could not give a definite reply —
Today, tomorrow, or a year to come.
(I was not used to such uncertainty.)

He shook his head. *It's been the same with me,
I've waited twenty years to go back home;
hopes raised, lies told, the broken promises;
and all the silences when no one came.*

I noticed then how grey the bare walls were.
A sheet of pegboard plugged the empty grate,
and there were smells of stale tobacco smoke
from others who, before us, had to wait.

Where are you from? he asked. Not far, I said.
We might have been close neighbours once
had years not intervened. I too have walked
the fields you knew, trod the same country lanes.

He did not answer that. The light grew darker still.
It was the kind of evening that is permanent;
a gloomy place with no one to explain
why both our trains were late — delayed, postponed.

And did you love the woman that I loved? he asked.
It's possible, I said, if we dispense with time.

His wild eyes looked beyond the window-pane —
there is no time in here, no calendar, no clocks;

All time is eternity. I've written that somewhere.
Now I am dead and longing to go back
to where I lived, whilst you are wishing
you could always stay where earth is kind —

the fens, you said? Not quite what I would choose.
I found my pleasure in those ancient hills
near Barnack, where the ancient stones
grew green and mellow in an autumn sun.

I tried to say it wasn't flatness I so much admired
as space and light. I longed for fields and sky
unhindered by the boundaries of man.
I sought horizons that could not be reached.

He laughed: *Always the unattainable!*
The one thing that I've learnt in my long life
is that one never should out-grow
what's measured by the cloth of one's own birth.

But what of fame? I asked. You have known that.
Did that not compensate for what the world
saw as your lack of privilege? There was reproach
and sadness in his slow reply: *I thought you knew,*

a burden comes with every song we write.
No praise or flattery is worth the price
we pay for stepping out of paradise.
I had a mind that once was full of light

until the stars were driven from my head
by those who claimed they understood
and, for my safety, locked me up... He paused.
And then, as if I were not there, began to sing:

Do letters reach beyond the grave?
Which wind will take them there?
Shall I rely upon the worms
to whisper in your ear?

Or should I tell that secret bird
the words I could not say
when we walked by the riverside
before the grief of snow?

If I could send these pages
by wing, or fire, or tree,
would you believe at last my dear
those unsaid words were true?

And should you share that company
where sorrows are unknown,
you'd know why I was silent.
Can such a love be sin?

Then, as his ghostly song came to an end,
four men stepped in with solemn tread
and stood before him as he wept: 'Your train
is coming, Mr Clare. Pick up your hat!'

He turned and waved a fragile hand:
It won't be long, he said. *Remember, time*
is in the mind, like pain or joy, or love;
we only ever mourn for what we cannot have.

They put him in his box, they carried him away.
I sensed a sudden chill where he had sat.
Then, knowing that I was alone again,
felt the cold hands of fear about my throat.

Chance

It would have been different
had the known answers never have given,
the unnecessary wounds opened
on the table he once thought was art.

It was the same for the man who was blind
before wisdom entered his mind,
or for the one who was locked
beyond the closed doors of all sound.

Even for those who never sought fame
but acted on the impulse of a dream,
(waiting at the corner of a street
to put an unknown face to a familiar voice)

there was the same irrational choice
that changed the chemistry of luck.
We like to call it fate if only to excuse
the possibilities we did not take.

It is the same with love.
There is an art in choosing who
shall be the sharer of its joys and hurts.
With every gift there is an element of chance.